THE PHOTOGRAPHS OF KANSAS STATE ATHLETICS

BY SCOTT D. WEAVER

For Patty, my biggest fan.

Special thanks to Don Zerbe, my assistant.

© 2011 Scott D. Weaver
The author retains sole copyright of the contributions to this book.

All rights reserved; no part of this publication may be reproduced, stored in a retrieval system, or transmitted in any form or by any means, electronic, mechanical, photocopying, recording, or otherwise without the prior written permission of the author.

INTRODUCTION

All Access is more than a collection of sports photos.

It is an opportunity for fans to participate in everything about Kansas State Athletics.

To enter the locker room.

To run onto the field.

To join in the huddle.

To perform with the K-State Marching Band.

To fly over fences on a Quarter Horse.

To race across Tuttle Creek Lake in a rowing boat.

To high jump over 7 feet.

To raise a championship trophy.

All Access is about the energy, emotion, pride and tradition that is Kansas State Athletics.

Eva Novotna and Petra Sedlmajerova,
April 5, 2000

Jonathan Beasley, October 7, 2000

Liz Wegner, October 14, 2000

Paulina Castillejos, April 22, 2001

Coach Mike Clark, April 22, 2001

Pat Maloney, April 28, 2001

Amanda Gigot, October 13, 2001

Erin Rees,
October 13, 2001

First novice eight,
October 15, 2001

Josh Scobey,
October 20, 2001

Chelsea Domenico, January 9, 2002

Queeneth Evurunobi, January 26, 2002

A.J. Elgert, April 16, 2002

COACH JENNY HALE, APRIL 17, 2002

Big 12 Outdoor Track and Field Champions, May 19, 2002

CHRISTINE BOUCHER,
AUGUST 31, 2002

MIRANDA SMITH, AUGUST 31, 2002

Marc Dunn,
September 14, 2002

Helmet, October 12, 2002

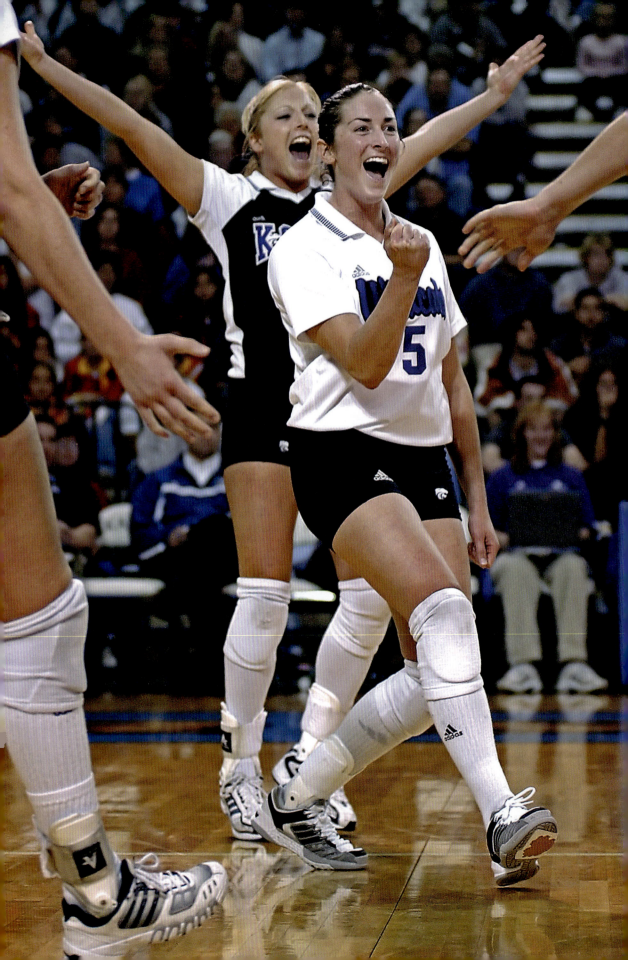

Rowing blades, November 2, 2002

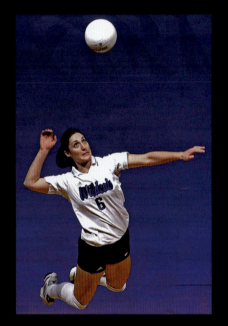

Jennifer Pollard, November 2, 2002

Opposite: Jami Sleichter and Laura Downey-Wallace, October 16, 2002

Football team, November 16, 2002

Ell Roberson, November 16, 2002

Terence Newman, November 23, 2002

Nicole Ohlde, December 7, 2002

Hayley McIver, April 12, 2003

Matt Van Cleave, May 17, 2003

Danny Morris, September 13, 2003

Josh Buhl, September 13, 2003

Darren Sproles, December 6, 2003

Laurie Koehn,
December 14, 2003

Women's basketball team, February 8, 2004

Megan Mahoney and Coach Deb Patterson, March 3, 2004

WILLIE THE WILDCAT AUTOGRAPH, APRIL 4, 2004

HIRAL BHAKTA, MAY 15, 2004

Lisa Martin, September 1, 2004

Kyle Lancaster, September 11, 2004

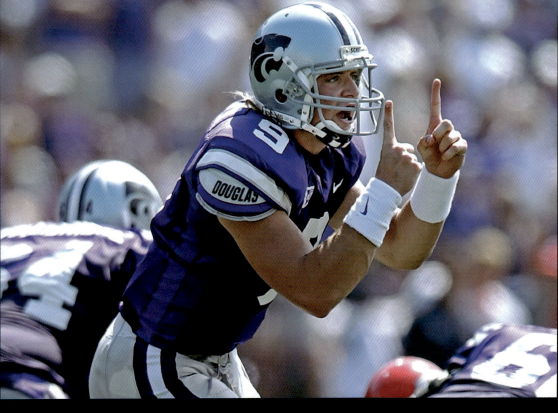

Dylan Meier, September 11, 2004

Power Cat flag, September 18, 2004

Coach Chris Cosh,
October 2, 2004

Coach Michael Smith,
October 2, 2004

Opposite: Jamie Perkins, October 6, 200

LINDSEY SALSBURY,
OCTOBER 9, 2004

GENTRY HORIGAN, NOVEMBER 13, 2004

Jeremiah Massey,
November 19, 2004

Coach Bob Elliott,
November 20, 2004

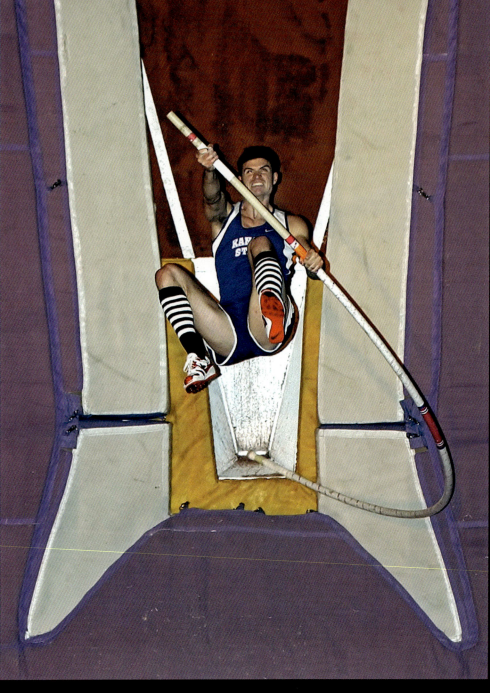
Wally Walstrom, January 14, 2005

Kendra Wecker, February 5, 2005

Brie Madden, February 16, 2005

First varsity eight, April 9, 2005

Fernanda Da Valle, April 17, 2005

Mathew Chesang, May 13, 2005

BREANNA EVELAND, MAY 15, 2005

Willie the Wildcat, September 3, 2005

KSU Stadium, October 8, 2005

Women's basketball team, January 4, 2006

Adam Reilly, January 7, 2006

Akeem Wright, January 11, 2006

Men's basketball team,
January 14, 2006

Coach Jimmy Elgas,
February 8, 2006

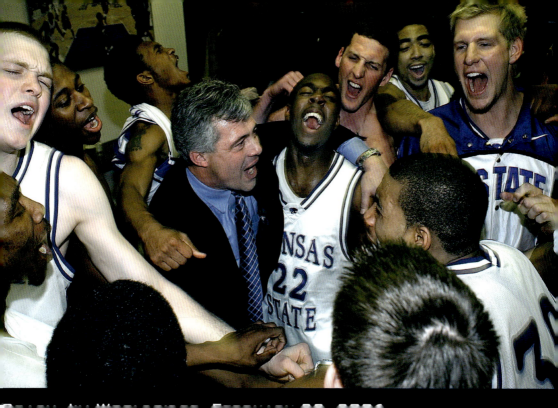

Brandon Farr, February 28, 2006

Summer Hamil, March 11, 2006

Casey Finnell, March 11, 2006

Bramlage Coliseum, March 31, 2006

Jessica McFarland and Danielle Zanotti, March 31, 2006

Opposite: WNIT Championship, March 31, 2006

Olga Klimova,
April 1, 2006

James Ball, April 22, 2006

Coach Patrick Sweeney, May 4, 2006

Christian Smith,
May 6, 2006

Laci Heller, May 6, 2006

Casey Becker,
May 6, 2006

Shunte Thomas, Lisi Maurer, Monique Coleman, May 6, 2006

Eleanor Burton, May 6, 2006

Kyle Yonke,
September 3, 2006

Mitchell Gregson, September 3, 2006

Rowing team house dedication, September 9, 2006

Football team, September 9, 2006

Coach Ron Prince,
September 9, 2006

Opposite: Bill Snyder Family Stadium, October 7, 2006

Willie the Wildcat, October 13, 2006

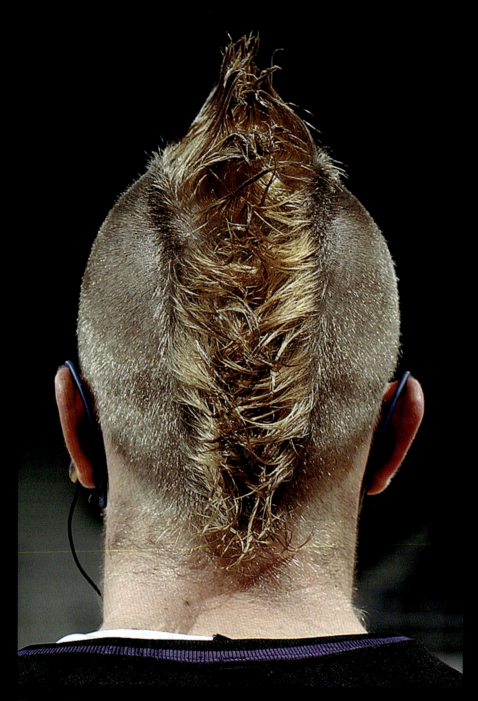

Ryan Patzwald, November 4, 2006

Coaches Deb Patterson and Kamie Ethridge, November 10, 2006

Coaches Brad Underwood and Bob Huggins, November 11, 2006

K-State defeats Texas, Bill Snyder Family Stadium, November 11, 2006

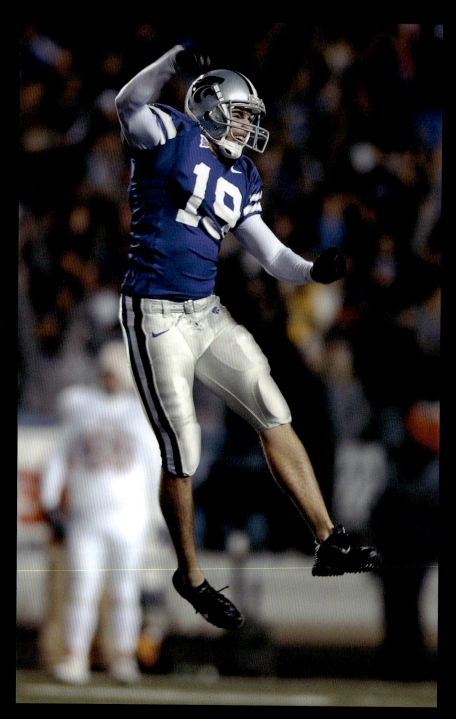

Jeff Snodgrass, November 11, 2006

Fans, November 18, 2006

Reggie Walker, November 18, 2006

MARLIES GIPSON, DECEMBER 17, 2006

Texas Bowl, December 28, 2006

Coach Bob Huggins,
January 31, 2007

Men's basketball team, January 31, 2007

Cartier Martin, March 3, 2007

BECKY ABRAMOVITZ,
MARCH 11, 2007

JANA LECHTENBERG, MARCH 11, 2007

OPPOSITE: ASHLEY COLLETT, MARCH 18, 2007

Bryce Bergman, April 20, 2007

Frank Murphy, April 21, 2007

Alex Umberger,
September 7, 2007

Taylor Coate, September 7, 2007

Wildcat Walk, September 8, 2007

Michael Beasley, November 3, 2007

Bill Walker, November 3, 2007

Jordy Nelson, November 10, 2007

Cheerleaders, November 11, 2007

Michael Beasley's shoes, November 29, 2007

Kelsey Chipman, Rita Liliom, Coach Suzie Fritz, Angie Lastra,
December 1, 2007

Shana Wheeler, January 16, 2008

Andre Gilbert,
January 19, 2008

Blake Young, January 19, 2008

Women's basketball team,
January 19, 2008

K-State defeats Kansas, Bramlage Coliseum,
January 30, 2008

Michael Beasley, January 30, 2008

Coach Frank Martin, January 30, 2008

Kimberly Dietz, March 1, 2008

CLENT STEWART, MARCH 4, 2008

DANIELLE ZANOTTI,
MARCH 5, 2008

RON ANDERSON,
MARCH 20, 2008

Coaches Bill Snyder and Casie Lisabeth, Sharon Snyder, March 29, 2008

Coach Steve Bietau, March 29, 2008

Morgan Campbell, March 30, 2008

Stephanie Hejde,
April 16, 2008

First varsity eight, April 30, 2008

Megan-Anne Perrin, May 3, 2008

Scott Sellers, May 3, 2008

Dane Yelovich, May 16, 2008

Nate Tenbrink, May 23, 2008

Jordan Bedore, Josh Freeman, Ian Campbell, Chris Carney, June 17, 2008

Volleyball team, September 13, 2008

Golf clubs,
September 22, 2008

Coach Kristi Knight,
September 23, 2008

Bridget Doyle,
October 3, 2008

Kayla Potter, October 3, 2008

Liz Godfrey,
October 17, 2008

Laura Browne,
October 17, 2008

Bramlage Coliseum, October 17, 2008

Shalee Lehning, October 17, 2008

Fans, October 25, 2008

Brandon Banks, November 1, 2008

Classy Cat, November 1, 2008

Coaches Jeff Grove and Suzie Fritz, November 1, 2008

Tennis team, November 7, 2008

Fans, November 14, 2008

Josh Freeman, November 15, 2008

CRAIG BOSWELL, NOVEMBER 22, 2008

COACH BILL SNYDER, NOVEMBER 24, 2008

DENIS CLEMENTE, NOVEMBER 25, 2008

Amanda Boor, December 13, 2008

Darren Kent, February 11, 2009

BRAMLAGE COLISEUM, FEBRUARY 14, 2009

Men's basketball team, February 14, 2009

Women's basketball team, February 15, 2009

Baseball team, April 11, 2009

Natasha Vieira and Mariya Slupska, April 18, 2009

First varsity eight, May 2, 2009

President Kirk Schulz, May 8, 2009

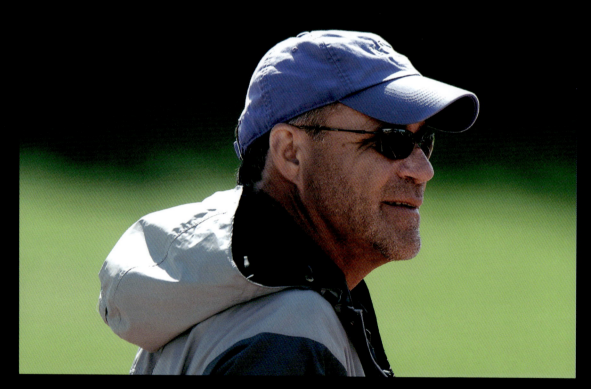
Coach Cliff Rovelto, May 9, 2009

Tom Pappas, May 9, 2009

Emmanuel Neizer, May 9, 2009

Tointon Family Stadium, May 15, 2009

President Kirk Schulz, John and Mary Lawrence Currie, May 18, 2009

Baseball team, May 29, 2009

Coach Brad Hill, June 1, 2009

Beverly Ramos, June 11, 2009

Eric Thomas, June 11, 2009

Loren Groves, June 12, 2009

K-State Marching Band, September 5, 2009

Bill Snyder Family Stadium, September 5, 2009

Coach Bill Snyder, September 5, 2009

Fort Riley Day, September 26, 2009

Abbi Sunner, September 28, 2009

Strength Coach Scott Greenawalt and Luis Colon,
October 7, 2009

BELLE, OCTOBER 17, 2009

Coach Suzie Fritz, November 8, 2009

Coach Frank Martin, January 12, 2010

Opposite: Ashley Sweat, November 16, 2009

Fans, January 12, 2010

ESPN College GameDay, January 30, 2010

Chris Merriewether and Dick Vitale, January 30, 2010

Bramlage Coliseum, February 17, 2010

BRAMLAGE COLISEUM, FEBRUARY 27, 2010

Mitchell Gregson, April 12, 2010

Brian Smoller, Abbi Sunner, Morgan Moon, May 3, 2010

Baseball Team, May 26, 2010

Daniel Thomas, June 1, 2010

Carson Coffman, July 22, 2010

Flag display at Bramlage Coliseum, September 11, 2010

Lauren Mathewson, September 25, 2010

Jacob Pullen and Curtis Kelly,
October 1, 2010

Bramlage Coliseum, October 15, 2010

Ahearn Field House, October 16, 2010

Rowers throw their coxswains in Tuttle Creek Lake, October 23, 2010

Fans, November 6, 2010

Football team plane, November 19, 2010

Men's basketball team, November 23, 2010

Pinstripe Bowl, December 30, 2010

Terrance Sweeney, December 30, 2010

Women's basketball team pink shoes, February 26, 2011